D0919092

LEARN ABOUT THE
GALAXY

by Golriz Golkar

Published by The Child's World®
1980 Lookout Drive • Mankato, MN 56003-1705
800-599-READ • www.childsworld.com

Design Elements: Shutterstock Images
Photographs ©: Shutterstock Images, cover (galaxy), cover (jar),
1 (galaxy), 1 (jar), 4 (glitter), 10, 18, 23; Africa Studio/Shutterstock
Images, 4 (oil); Elizabeth A. Cummings/Shutterstock Images, 4
(food coloring); Rick Orndorf, 5; CXC/SAO;IR & UV:NASA/JPL-
Caltech/NASA/STScI/NASA, 6; Detlef Hartmann/CXC/SAO/
JPL-Caltech/NASA, 9; Alex Mit/Shutterstock Images, 13; NASA
images/Shutterstock Images, 14; JPL-Caltech/NASA, 17; ESA/
The Hubble Heritage Team (STScI/AURA)/NASA, 21

Copyright © 2020 by The Child's World®
All rights reserved. No part of this book may be reproduced or
utilized in any form or by any means without written permission
from the publisher.

ISBN 9781503832183
LCCN 2018962836

Printed in the United States of America
PA02420

About the Author

Golriz Golkar is a teacher and children's author who lives in Nice, France. She enjoys cooking, traveling, and looking for ladybugs on nature walks.

TABLE OF CONTENTS

CHAPTER 1

Let's Create a Galaxy!

MATERIALS

- ☐ Glass jar with lid
- ☐ Baby oil
- ☐ Mixing bowl
- ☐ Water
- ☐ Blue food coloring
- ☐ Red food coloring (optional)
- ☐ Glitter

It is a good idea to gather your materials before you begin.

The glitter and bubbles look like the stars and planets.

STEPS

1. Fill the jar halfway with baby oil.

2. Combine $\frac{1}{2}$ cup water with two drops of food coloring in a bowl. You can use blue food coloring. You can also mix red and blue to make purple.

Many galaxies can only be seen with
powerful scientific equipment.

3. Add the water to the oil.

4. Add some glitter.

5. Close the jar tightly. Carefully shake it back and forth. The oil bubbles and glitter look like stars. Enjoy your galaxy!

CHAPTER 2

What Is a Galaxy?

A galaxy is a giant group of stars, dust, and gases. The center is called a **nucleus**. The nucleus pulls everything towards it. **Gravity** holds the galaxy together. In the experiment, the bubbles and glitter make up a galaxy.

The nucleus keeps the whole galaxy together.

The universe began after the Big Bang explosion.

There are billions of galaxies in the universe. They formed after the **Big Bang**. This huge explosion created the universe 13.8 billion years ago. Heat, energy, and **particles** exploded from a pebble-sized mass. The particles expanded within seconds. They cooled down. Stars, galaxies, and other space objects were formed from the particles.

DID YOU KNOW?

Scientists still don't know what caused the Big Bang. They are still trying to learn where the mass came from.

CHAPTER 3

What's Inside a Galaxy?

Galaxies have different sizes. Small galaxies contain less than one billion stars. Large galaxies have up to 100 trillion stars. Galaxies also contain planets. Earth is found in the Milky Way Galaxy. The Sun and other planets of our **solar system** are part of the Milky Way.

We live in the Milky Way Galaxy.

Galaxies contain clouds of gases called **nebulae**. The gases in a nebula are very hot. The particles in the clouds are pulled together by gravity. The gases get hotter as the particles get closer together. The particles combine when they get hot enough. This becomes a star. Some galaxies are always producing new stars. Others stopped making them long ago.

The gases in nebulae combine to form stars.

Every large galaxy has a **black hole** at its nucleus. A black hole forms when a star is dying out. The gravity that formed the star continues to pull on the gases. The particles continue to combine. The star runs out of energy. The star collapses and **implodes**. Gravity is very strong. Not even light and particles can escape a black hole.

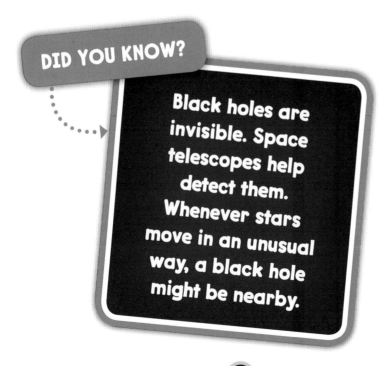

DID YOU KNOW?

Black holes are invisible. Space telescopes help detect them. Whenever stars move in an unusual way, a black hole might be nearby.

Black holes are invisible, but scientists can observe the dust and gas that swirl into them.

Galaxies also contain **dark matter**. Dark matter does not give off light. It does not have a clear shape. Scientists can tell dark matter affects gravity. They are still trying to discover what makes up dark matter.

If you are far away from towns and bright lights, you can see the Milky Way at night.

Our galaxy is large. It contains 100 billion stars. It has enough gases to make billions of more stars. It has a massive black hole. The Milky Way is around 13.6 billion years old. It was one of the first galaxies to form after the Big Bang.

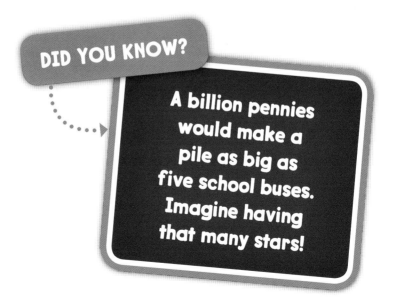

DID YOU KNOW?

A billion pennies would make a pile as big as five school buses. Imagine having that many stars!

CHAPTER 4

What Kinds of Galaxies Are There?

Spiral galaxies contain old and new stars. They are flat disks. They spin fast around the nucleus in a spiral movement. The Milky Way is a spiral galaxy.

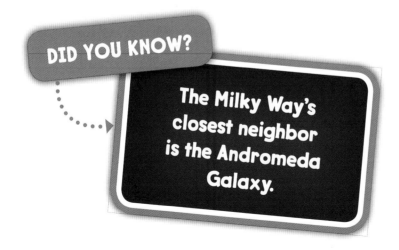

DID YOU KNOW?

The Milky Way's closest neighbor is the Andromeda Galaxy.

Some galaxies do not have clear shapes.

Elliptical galaxies are shaped like stretched out circles. They contain many old stars. They rotate around the nucleus. New stars rarely form.

Irregular galaxies are not spiral nor elliptical. They are pulled by the gravity of nearby galaxies. They lack a clear shape.

Glossary

Big Bang (BIG BANG) The Big Bang was a massive cosmic explosion that created the universe billions of years ago. Many stars and galaxies formed after the Big Bang.

black hole (BLAK HOL) A black hole is a space inside the nucleus of a galaxy formed from a collapsed star. Gravity inside a black hole is so strong that light cannot escape.

dark matter (DARK MAT-er) Dark matter is made of invisible particles inside galaxies. Dark matter does not give off light and cannot be seen.

gravity (GRAV-i-tee) Gravity is the force a planet or other body in space uses to draw objects toward its center. Gravity on Earth keeps objects from floating away.

implodes (im-PLOHDS) An object implodes when it collapses inward. A star implodes to form a black hole.

nebulae (NEB-yuh-lay) Nebulae are clouds of gas found in galaxies. The gasses in nebulae are used to form stars.

nucleus (NOO-klee-uhs) The nucleus is the central part of something around which other parts are gathered. The center of a galaxy is its nucleus.

particles (PART-i-culls) Particles are tiny pieces of something. Stars are made when particles in gasses combine.

solar system (SOH-ler SIS-tuhm) The solar system is the Sun, its eight planets, and all other bodies that orbit it. The Sun is at the center of the solar system.

universe (YOO-nuh-vurss) The universe is all matter and space in existence. Stars, planets, and dark matter are all found in the universe.

To Learn More

In the Library

Buckley Jr., James. *Stars and Galaxies*.
New York, NY: DK Publishing, 2017.

Rector, Rebecca Kraft. *Galaxies*. New York,
NY: Enslow Publishing, 2019.

Sabatino, Michael. *20 Fun Facts about Galaxies*.
New York, NY: Gareth Stevens Publishing, 2015.

On the Web

Visit our website for links about galaxies:
childsworld.com/links

*Note to Parents, Teachers, and Librarians: We routinely verify our Web links to make
sure they are safe and active sites. So encourage your readers to check them out!*

Index